# oil spell

PREVIOUS WORK

*MOUTHS* (NOEMI PRESS, 2017)

# oil spell

## claire marie stancek

OMNIDAWN PUBLISHING
RICHMOND, CALIFORNIA
2018

Cover art: Original artwork by Ruben Briseno Reveles
www.rubenreveles.com

Cover typeface: Kabel LT Std & Perpetua Std
Interior typeface: Perpetua Std

Cover & interior design by Cassandra Smith

Special thanks to Steve Halle for design support.


Offset printed in the United States
by Edwards Brothers Malloy, Ann Arbor, Michigan
On 55# Enviro Natural 100% Recycled 100% PCW
Acid Free Archival Quality FSC Certified Paper


Library of Congress Cataloging-in-Publication Data

Names: Stancek, Claire Marie, author.
Title: Oil spell / Claire Marie Stancek.
Description: Richmond, California : Omnidawn Publishing, 2018.
Identifiers: LCCN 2017052620 | ISBN 9781632430557 (softcover)
Classification: LCC PS3619.T36473 A6 2018 | DDC 811/.6--dc23
LC record available at https://lccn.loc.gov/2017052620


Published by Omnidawn Publishing, Oakland, California
www.omnidawn.com    (510) 237-5472    (800) 792-4957
10  9  8  7  6  5  4  3  2  1
ISBN: 978-1-63243-055-7

in memory of my Baba Yaga

Jaroslava Blažková
1933-2017

//│ {invoke _night*[spell]


happened that night escaped from the menagerie
song fragment happened night escaped
spread " "evil

like butter like birds
wet with blood smacking into glass
night escaping             Medusa's hair into light

like obscene infinity : evil
they say is that
which is unintelligible or  [[it threatens to return forever        live

arrived what continues
to haunt us a : dream that could only have been _dreamt in dark/burgeon
bruised in somnambulance bruising : impious : holding a book

and a gun the gun covered
in words the book
covered in oil the oil

was riot or the color
of what magically survives its physical annihilation
which is riot and it spoke //

__the borders you recognize will consume you
women who are evil are said to be "possessed"
*for what are you searching*

bite the head of a live dick
rubs sticks/stones together
song fragment covered] in oil

a new night more dark                          is take

and what it does                               place take

in the world                                   places take

7

over created ungod /night
sun goes out ++with it the stars and happened
masscrash in dark all the planes felled dark downing

masscrash dark trainscrash in utter night
demonic myth model
darkness spreads fucks       up borders between things

what were rhythmic and periodic textures of human life
spirit attack : become : indistinguishable : a spectral dimension
similar enchantments among remote ancestors

winged with an owl's feathers|| holding a book and a gun
for what are you searching says night
trance be on you somnambulance

security camera happened
that a blue horse escaped
like what was the idea of nature

escaped the night
their hearts burned( their limbs trembling
barbed_with a thorn +continues to haunt masscrash

outer darkness come inner everyone
on the sidewalk masscrash cease
rest what //you were seeking arrived already dark pull

spilled inglorious fruit ^no light
yawn of the night
invoke what is already gone

[spill]


outer darkness come inner everyone
bite the head of a live dick
they say is that
women who are evil are said to be "possessed"
spilled inglorious fruit ^no light
security camera happened

what were rhythmic and periodic textures of human life
of what magically survives its physical annihilation
masscrash dark trainscrash in utter night
bruised in somnambulance bruising : impious : holding a book
sun goes out ++with it the stars and happened


similar enchantments among remote ancestors

escaped the night
__the borders you recognize will consume you
in the world places take
trance be on you somnambulance
spread " "evil
masscrash in dark all the planes felled dark downing
barbed_with a thorn +continues to haunt masscrash
spirit attack : become : indistinguishable : a spectral dimension
arrived what continues
happened that night escaped from the menagerie
rubs sticks/stones together
was riot or the color

their hearts burned( their limbs trembling


to haunt us a : dream that could only have been _dreamt in dark/burgeon

that a blue horse escaped
wet with blood smacking into glass

over created ungod /night
in words the book
yawn of the night

song fragment covered] in oil
and what it does place take
on the sidewalk masscrash cease

and a gun the gun covered
like butter like birds
night escaping Medusa's hair into light
song fragment happened night escaped

demonic myth model

which is unintelligible or [[it threatens to return forever          live

which is riot and it spoke //

covered in oil the oil

rest what //you were seeking arrived already dark pull


for what are you searching
winged with an owl's feathers | | holding a book and a gun
for what are you searching says night
like what was the idea of nature

darkness spreads fucks up borders between things

a new night more dark is take

like obscene infinity : evil
invoke what is already gone

fang vision spell
chirrup cluck corpse flower chew

caw snarl a maw blares/bares its teeth
snawrl caw seeing/bleating mouth and teeth
(me/I) speak from inside a gullet (mitted / thout / not, a / xtrem)       '

clatter-grunt cunt up what noise arrived in fog chew-chew
veer squeaking tooth to bone ligaments lineaments
line garments grunt squawk I/you was wolfed

fang vision spell
chirrup
*corpse flower what noise made*

we shriek perch / we shriek —pdeeer ohwowowo
wings yip wings from wall to word wings shriek
take back mad u made madm madmess

☽

*/ / luxuriant shade ; INFESTNEST / /*    TRINGA
*winding shores and passing sails / / tranquil*    OCHRÓPUS GREEN
*beauty grandeur* [[[FESTN    towers crumble &


*the bat, still flittings of*    decompose into
your population trend is (not) known    not    nightmoon
believed    to be decreasing,    us of us ,    runs up the sky


the rest of us who were in range , ranging    obscured SANDPIPER

☽

come back PHYLLOSCOPUS
*while the twilight still overpowered* TROCHILOIDES
*the light of the moon* GREENISH
book was crawling it , infested it , WARBLER by
was pus-slick & branches towers
crusted was all golden & broken
alive come back golden breaking
*but the moon came out* SXCL RBTR

☽

leeching ligaments blighting [bleeding] WHNCHT CHLDNS

*At about 2120 hours, US Drone* HYBRD WHSKRD
*carried out missile strike* TRN into nightarms
*killed militants also* obscured by branches
*include a 12 year old child* time's moonface
*lower part of the ruin, the cliff* glows terrestrial
*on which it stood* CARRION CROW

☽

goodbye *the moonlight*    SYLVIA
*lay upon the hills like snow*    ATRICAPILLA

*more than the light of day* goodbye    BLACKCAP

☽

*Attack on village US Drone carried*   NYCTICORAX
*out missile strike*   NYCTICORAX
*at a suspected*   BLACK-CROWNED
*vehicle near Hassu*   NIGHT-HERON
*Khel Bridge*   suddenly lights &

woke into fog    moon too in fog & blurred   suddenly
the moon & again the moon goodbye   lights recognize litter

*the moon was behind* come back   dropped in a past/ life
*sweet and gentle nest // hour*   ACCIPITER
*and the scenery awakened*   BREVIPES LEVANT

☽

fecund cells fetid selfs unshelving opening  stale hot
into ~~opening~~ noise  subway air say
our become or  sublunary

unbordered clot living [among them  lives interfere
seep now  in carrion [care?]  machine
what we seethe we seethe together  swirl the interior

murk sweat mingling  ate now  rot bog  SPARROWHAWK
knit in  marl  mire in I  blur  EMBERIZA PUSILLA

*Amongst killed, three were / / veiled in white,*  smoke refuge
*issued from the cloisters no nest*  while echoes turn
*whitened by the light of the moon,*  in a quiet language

airborne  LITTLE BUNTING

☽

*. small grated window, gleamed with red glow*      thorns you
*west which // like wood-tops &waves lower*          text me & my
*still , , twilight            several*              mood CLDRS BRD
*by moonlight goodbye*                               BRD'S SNDPPR

*low murmur of waves, breaking*                      MLNCRYPH BMCLT
*on the shore // melancholy dashing of oars*         BMCLTD LRK
*feebly from a distance*                             LOXIA

*Among five killed, two are reportedly*             changes breaks
*foreigners and two children.*                      through  branches

☽

herds of cattle of : pastures were animated [    breaksCURVIROSTR
beautiful cream-colour; the nest is in a tree    A RED CROSSBILL
cavity, either a natural hole or one    RED KNOT
excavated by two missiles fired from drone    AHEAMTPUOS
insects, spiders, small mammals malleable,    ADEMAELIODW
depending on availability    mood

shattered battlements , some    across   sky clouds
sea-fowl , the extended    running quick  breathe
wings of / / illumined    lights ANCRAIAN
by sun, the upward    ARTCEHYCOSTER
beams of / / disk was now sunk : horizon    & the air among them

At 2050 hours, US Drone carried out    PIED FLYCATCHER
missile strike AN @NGEL OF LIGHT ,    a laugh haunts
ENCOMPASSED BY FIENDS    me pealing rhyme

☽

come joine us in the muck    headlights

, wooded steppe, assailants,    STRIX NEBULOSA
gorges, overgrown quarries come,    GREAT
farmland with rocky areas or cliffs    GREY OWL
come & open forest & taiga    CARDUELIS
& two missiles come    CANNABINA

US DRONE    swing the corner honks

05 [U} 03 WE 02 US    staccato I am

*with enormous round towers, buttresses*    in noise    with one
*of proportionable strength,*    EURASIAN LINNET
*arch of the large gate Two missiles a series*    REMIZ
*of flaps followed*    glove off    on
*by glide with wings held in dihedral*    a cellphone love's

☽

stream , course of / / under the shades :   PENDULINUS
overhung its grassy margin   EURASIAN

On the night between 2009 at about   PENDULINE-TIT
0200 hours, four missiles were fired from Drone   in nightblur   strophic
a pleasant moonlight evening, but not   wires careen
clear come back   above my   tangle

was seen a ruined watch-tower / / a point of   ALECTORIS
rock / / sea / / tufted   CHUKAR CHUKAR
foliage , rising from among   FULICA ATRA

she rose in uncommon majesty over the sea,   marking  thought's range
slowly ascending through the clouds wait   running too  far

☽

it was a lovely moonlight night goodbye   COMMON COOT

21

☽

when we came in sight of our own dear Grasmere   ALCA TORDA R

anxious interval >>examining ruin / /   AZORBILL LARUS
walking environs *all over the sky sonic  the vale   ARMENICUS
looked fair and quiet   ARMENIAN GULL
in the moonshine, the Church was there and all   dizzy crooked
the cottages come back   telephone booth

of a brilliant yellow hue   marked "bell"　here

nest is a gluttonous hollow on dry   BUCEPHALA
ground nest covetous   ISLANDICA
gorge near water nest is teething and drool   rings　empty
in the open nest   signal you do
numbmumbling under the cover   not call
of driftwood nest   BARROW'S
madgrass hummocks   GOLDENEYEsnot
and hillocks or rocks Strict legislation   slip and pus
on oil exploration and transportation strict   puss=sliming
feeding on spiders   scab=wind the
a shelter of cells feeding   tarn=your venom
on the shelter airborne   yarn=your vein

☽

surveyed vastness // ruins // fancy bore her back          lights the phrase hand
            to past ages :"And these walls,"          on her cheek blue
                        now mortal remains          turn a corner




☽

                        US Drone          LCSTLL LNCLT



            sun had left earth = twilight darken          they throw a fragment
            the mountains // distant waters,          of litter across
            amphibian bane reflecting          my mystical path I feel
the blush glowed in the west // line of light,          moon's LNCLTD
            skirting the horizon          WRBLR SPLPL
wait at once the clouds seemed to cleave          SNGLNSS LGHNG
            asunder, and left her in the centre          absence
                        of a black-blue vault          like a magnet

☽

in moonlight the land opened open
sewage open fermenting buzzing  w
innumerable        wings        devils
                wings of        diarrhea
winds slop    in moonlight [goodbye]
    mouths mauled            in mutual
tooth tongue amphibian toad    discord
some  one scratching    skin in mire
            the sound    scratching
                    made  wealing
    whining    writhing    sound
reached into  vulvas    into  wax
    vexed    sound edged    wriggled
            horde pressed
    scrabbled and sneaked        and
        the throng    palpitated
in        moonlight    throbbing lesion
        legion    the land then
    was mere    sluice  & cyst

slobber creature
in mixed light splayed
all  directions
/ screeching
hurrying graffiti
drips down a heart
mine malignancy / what
&    not mine
cobwebs on st francis
street dregs of frenzy
surge under a store
called cloak & dagger
he is a fucking brat/
but he's happy
snout wails
moon over-shining
sign repeating OPEN
streetcar CLDRS
TMMNCK

luxuriant woods, with which they abounded
? sequester this spot from the world

GLRD THKL THKL
LRK

24

☽

*perceived the Gothic remains of an abbey : rude*   PRS LGBRS SMBR TT
*lawn, overshadowed // spreading trees*   TRDS PHLMLS SNG
*coeval with the building // diffused*   THRSH

*there were two stars beside her, that twinkled*   honks staccato
*in and out, and seemed almost like*   I am in noise
*butterflies in motion and lightness* goodbye   with one glove  off
. pharmaceutical night [[   FRAETRAUCL

☽

nest a shallow scrape nest a thin
lining in thick vegetation nest near shallow
pools lakes broad slow-flowing rivers nest emergent
littoral vegetation breed
pondweeds nest
coastal delta areas in open moist low-lying
sedge-grass or moss-lichen
nest in tree
holes hollow stumps nest from forestry
management, which has resulted
in the loss of hollow
and broken trees which provide nest
these stars grew
and diminished as they passed from, or
went into, the clouds wait

ARCCTIA
ATLANTIC PUIFFN
loping   wheeling
clattering in/ noise
EMBERIZA CIRLUS
towers decompose into
frosted glass & frost
CIRL BUNTING
MOTACILLA rots into
nightair a copcar
at a swerved angle
CITREOLA CITRINE
WAGTAIL
TURDUS MERULA
driver seat door swung

☽

*At about 1830 hours, US nest carried out*     open suspended
*missile strike*     stale air seeps

*a very mild nest night* wait     copcar night

smell of burning plastic :

in columns coursing

new life

at the side of the road

sprouting

human life

newspaper pile

of light

bass beats

dusts in dust

new sounds

new life

dusty air

head crushed

body still perfect

life cans

murder

blood

meet at one point

music

cold hands

new

light

dead snake

rubber

cans rusted

multiple, not

"language"

columns

life

in human

gravel path

sounds

branches in branches

creatures

air bodies

gun life

"hearts burning"

what pattern of tile

teeming molt

water

wars

burgeoning

turning

yearning

winged

new

drill

a key

of time, what

new life

boarded

life

ant throng:

oil forest

winged

breathers

requirement

dimly

swinging wires

drought life

sand-filled, burning

water

whose

a key in the door

gravel path

fang vision spell
spoked out from earth and heavy
chirrup cluck corpse

what the wings made mad was SNARL was
SING CHURR was (ficant / nuted / here / is not / red, an / *sensus*)
woah what made i/you was a needle a thread a name : wolfed

fang vision spell
*corpse chew in noise what made | { flesh remnant*

you/WE) came down(up) to the street to see (paus / een boo / ,
as he / nscious / eat imp) gutter grates been torn (born) what fishes
went coursing the median : a red flashing bracket a

salmon tears the blood (brihgt) from the sun
red (umber / matte adm) memory new way was
made on ways : concrete where concrete stays

fang vision spell
chirrup cluck corpse flower chew
*bark bark bark bark bark , , , , bark*

neither but both/ and between space of fang & voiced
flesh-growl bray-sob & BLAST half blast
half bay half pipe half calf cheep wheeping, monster (aclf) combust

JUG BAY SING ! (snarl spell "snarl") & a wheeping
whing hinged what opened : what this hting

(sting) opened : what opened : to be / *on sente* / *ation*

☽

chldns lcptrs wht-wngd trn
lyrurus tetrix black grouse milvus
migrans black kite

down the towers mine
& not mine under a
store called cloak &


plegadis falcinellus glossy ibis aquila
chrysaetos golden eagle

dagger CALIDRIS
PUGNAX


parus montanus willow tit
zapornia pusilla baillon's crakeclamator
glandarius great
spotted cuckoo dendrocopos major
great spotted
woodpecker neophron erpcnosreput
egyptian evuutrl cygnus olor
mute swan
morus bassanus northern
gannet strcrrs pmrns pmrn jgr prnll clrs
rdd's ccntr

RUFF
APUS PALLIDUS
PALLID GREAT
WHITE EGRET evil
embryo with mud
blisters | what din you
erupt | what ash you
spray | on this churlish
girl you rush
by but it's not you
dots in tar

☽

wait the moonlump overcast     constellations over

maximum security *in hollows or depressions*     the sidewalk a child's
*in trees, in rock ledges or steep*     SWIFT LOXIA
*stream banks, normally*     blank stare pattern
*near water*     where signs   shine

☽

*At about 1015 hours, four (04) missiles*   DROUGHT
*were fired from US Drone over Bobar*   DRINKER >


☽

goodbye *beautiful new moon over* nest   WANT

*At about 2150 hours, a US drone attack was*   WRENCHER >
*carried out and fired two missiles*   BLEED OIL
*// had once supported the*   HORDE > WENT >
*roof*PATHOGENMICROBECELCELLCE   WEND >
*AIR*   WILT, DELICIOUS

*monastery of St. Claire // near the margin*   SWAMP
*of the sea : cliffs, suddenly sinking*   MEMBRANE

☽

*DEEP STRUCK / WITH AWE / DOME*
*O'ERTHROWN THEY MARKED /*
*BEAUTY BLOOM'D : THE CASTLE'S*
*MOULD'RING TOWERS*
*DECAY'D 2100 hours, rsdntl cmpnd ws*
*trgtd wth fr gdd mssls frm S Drn t Nshp Mr*
*_Khn r f Thsl Ldh, S. W.gncy. Dtls r wtd.*

DV iualqa enalpisins
esptpe aegle bark of
staples crusted
rusted newspaper bins
lashed PNIUGIUSN
EMNPSINI GREAT
KAU

*nght-brds, lw nd dsml htng f / / rstd mng :*
*vyd bttlmnts f th rn / /*
*wt mn crscnt*

PODICEPS together in
chains
in moonlight solar

☽

*At about 0100*　　CRISTATUS GREAT

*hours (at night) 02 01 04 01*　　CRESTED GREBE
*Awoman will killed and all*　　NHALOYC
*the . missile were fired from Drone*　　MSYRENSNIS panels
*injured were kids as reported. two*　　drink　pale
*missiles were fired*　　dreams　start　awake
*from Drone*　　man's ghost WHITE-
*over a vehicle took up // along*　　DBSETAER
*the passage // another*　　INKFGISREH AGVAI
*door: unlocked, descended : a few steps // into*　　DAAMSII YELLOW-
*a chapel in ruins*　　IBLLED

☽

industrialized farming practices, abuse and
solitude, secret domestic, agricultural
intensification, ground clearance, excessive
use of toxic chemicals and road traffic
deaths lacking snow cover

face leaning forward
from   night window
parked car I LONO,
BRANTA
LEUCOPSIS

electrocution and airplane strikes shepherds
with guns *ON THE GRASS UNDER*
*THE SHADE OF SOME HIGH TREES*
*NEAR THE RUINS*

BARNACLE GOOSE
CORVUS CORONE
hurry into  construction
cones   overturned

slopes and gorges and crags with patches
of snow : ropes and
gore lacking snow
cover : some herb and grass
cover : range
and rearrange :

fiend of lumpy veins :
what feeble flow you
exude : what relics
welter offices
decompose into empty
illumination after

*range size has not been quantified,*
*but it is not believed to approach*
*the thresholds for Vulnerable*
*under the population size*
*criterion lofty promontory, terminated*
*by a // summit whose / , impending*
*over waves / crowned // ruined tower*

*degradation and pile , the*
*greater part of loss,*
*appeared to be sinking into*
*RUINS, // about 0330*
*hours, US Drone*
the workingday long
ceiling lights

mump thing creaking
dripping mongrel
thing stray thing OTIS
TARDA GREAT BUSTARD
PHALACROCORAX CARBO
GREAT CORMORANT
cesspool thronging with distended skins,
the very pores of which will dribble moan
atop a heap of bodies a creature will stand
on a mass of leg stumps a gristle creature
in putrescence shake its scabs at wind
its words will make a quagmire listen by
magma words juice-water creature in
language contagion in

harsh across
*had withstood the*
*ravages of time*
*petroleum pollution, peat*
*extraction,* I am
wandering   after hours
in light    makes
everything //
remaining features ?
fabric more awful in
decay *the burning and*
*mowing of reeds and*
*eutrophication* carried
out missile strike

PICUS CANUS GREY-FACED
WOODPECKER ANSER ANSER
GREYLAG GOOSE

we are   (aren't we)
at a tilt CRISTATUS
GREAT CRESTED

☽

*walking in the woods // hung on a*    the morass where this
*promontory ? overlooking the sea*    gargoyle hunches two

*it was a fine wild moonlight night* come back    cops lean heavy into
*woods receding disclosed // summits of*    their guns
*the Pyrenees // distant USDRONE*    towers empty will
*missile strike*    sicken #

*wide prospect of sea and land // sun now*    themselves into night
*setting Pyrenees*    their spirits flee
*walked by moonlight* come back    stench cleft you

*8 female 05 children 07 male all civilians*    & become stars

☽

*Two missile were fired Drone*    IT LAYS IN THE
*on a private premise*    ABANDONED NEST
*in village [hunts from a perch, dropping*    bike bell key
*down to take prey from branches or the ground]*    jangle step rustle hands
*air of solemnity / / so strongly*    in pockets   OF
*characterized the pile*    OTHER BIRDS
*;— mountains spiral summits of, touched with*    OF PREY, ON
*a purple tint of, broken*    BROKEN TREE
*and steep above*    "hey"    chimes the
*emptiness / / forced back the gate, heavy with*    moon still SNAGS,
*iron work / / creaked harshly*    SOMETIMES

☾

& who among us is satisfied     towers like dreams I
   with her own designs     don't   recognize

☽

*body of the invertebrate, / / one of those*
*ancient fortresses, that, from age*
*and neglect,*
*had fallen to decaymported pigs,*
*monkeys and rats*
*fed on the eggs in their*
*ground nests*
*lofty battlements, thickly enwreathed with*
*ivy / / half demolished, birds of prey ,*
*residence of*

*ON A MISTLETOE*
*BROOM, OR*
*RARELY IN A*
beckoning off kilter
rhythm finger
*SHALLOW*
snapping exhalation
*DEPRESSION AT*
*THE FOOT* from
rooftop greywhite

*recently extinct gluttonous mump muncher*
*Drone at about 1600 hours upon a 08 09 08*
*residential house*

night mist *OF A*
*TREE BROKEN*
falling & rising

☽

*The loss of nest holes from the felling of old hollow*
*trees and the restoration of old buildings is also*
*likely to affect the species had, in truth, no*
*philosophy that could render her calm to such losses*
*let me hope I shall not live to mourn the loss of those*
*who are dearer to me than life she was compelled to*
*resign herself to the loss of it 'my loss I know can*
*never be recovered' let me not lament more than ever*
*the loss of such parents I am at a loss, madam the*
*punishment, which is my due, the loss of you and*
*she fretted for the loss of her, I fancy, but she never*
*told me so and, perceiving, that she had fainted*
*probably from loss of blood, ran for water;*

against moon
*TREE SNAGS,*
*SOMETIMES ON A*
*MISTLETOE*
a truck rumbles
*BROOM, OR*
*RARELY* air's still
tangled I thought
you heard me I
jumped at the sound
*IN A SHALLOW*
*DEPRESSION AT*
*THE FOOT OF A*

*natural vista : country , view of the, / /*
*terminated by hills } faded blue horizon*

*TREE FURRY*
*PETALLED*

☽

'We are near the monastery, then,'   SKYSPREAD these

USDRONE at about 1330 hourse targeted   things as sounds

O3 missiles were fired from a Drone over   move over with one
the procession O PASSER DOMESTICUS   continuous nest
HOUSE SPARROW PHYLLOSCOPUS   alongside us & decompose
IBERICUS IBERIAN CHIFFCHAFF   faster than our flesh
PUFFINUS LHERMINIERI AUDUBON'S   clutches nests was
SHEARWATER FRINGILLA TEYDEA   chequewring the errth,
BLUE CHAFFINCH ARENARIA   which also decomposes
INTERPRES RUDDY TURNSTONE   into love into

TSRTPEOPEAIL TRUTUR EUROPEAN   towers empty nests was
TURTEL-OVDE ORIOLUS ORIOLUS   airborne nsaer rthyrepous
EURASIAN GOLDEN ORIOLE   lesser white-
PLUVIALIS APRICARIA EURASIAN   rfotned goose
GOLDEN PLOVER PICUS VIRIDIS   balconies filled with
EURASIAN GREEN WOODPECKER   tables bikes

FALCO SUBBUTEO EURASIAN HOBBY   & dead potted plants
STT TPHRNT STRN RCK-NTHTCH   BLACKBIRD
ZTHR DM RSN SCLY THRSH   PYRRHULA

☽

moonlimp, but it rained come back MEROPS APIASTER
*4/5 Missile attack 22 persons died 26 09 26* BEE-EATER
*At about 1500 hours, US Drone carried out* GOLDFINCH
*missile strike at a house* swept leaves
*At about 1615 hours, US Drone carried out* swept by wind
*missile strike* your thought

☽

*At 1215 hours, US Drone carried*  RDL RLLDS SQCC
*out missile strike*  HRN CLMB NS
*the sky looked threatening* common nkigfisher  pushes into my head I
gvaia mmire common nolo ytayha ranife  fight it then
common ahorpcd  it becomes STCK DV

*On the night at 2303 hours,*  SYLVIA UNDATA
*Drone carried out missiles attack at the*  DARTFORD
*house of one Afghan Refugee*  WARBLER

☽

come back *"O, the unutterable darkness of*   me takes
*the sky, and the earth below the moon, and*   me in as I take it
*the glorious brightness of the moon itself!"*   abounding/ litter
*dimly, but it was a grey cloudy night* goodbye   FUERTEVENTURA


*a sound of many voices, slowly chanting,*   STONECHAT my/
*arose from within*   heart

fang vision spell
roar & gabble drench chewed [ being chewed chirrup

chirpjugbreeerwoo-it !chirpjug after the flood slicked
stone became skin not : (excess) for long but

for a time : a flash : a flesh said ERR SONG *cack-cack

fang vision spell
*weeping sung  / out strings gobbed*

vocifer luce lucif blast (me / I) received – I remain, WEW-wew
CHEW-CHEW roar  $$ monster fang blast
(into / bitten / will cow / the eve / a sour / this he)

pipe screams were scathed under under : in
slabs – there under where you / she slavered (sat) (assion / ficientl
/ pens w / "suffer / , but t) message what remains

spores     viral     gas

ball     spreading     wire

year     burning     sing

swing     whoop     spreading

red     ball     gas

flu     spreading     dimly

spore     gas     wing

spreading     near     cough

boil     water     coil

| | | |
|---|---|---|
| bees | new | polyurethane |
| new | burn | new |
| PVC | new | pattern |
| new | polypropylene | new |
| rash | new | mosquito |
| new | corn | new |
| sound | new | polycarbonate |
| new | seed | new |

🌙

slowly chanting, a sound of many voices
drained into the sky     night blight walked
by moonlight goodbye hemorrhaged by
starlight hello where she stepped gunk and
sludge frothed where she sat an inflamed
moon hung : an : incubus : in : a : ringing
: sky she          was searching for the
trenches    where her son   ridges where
her createdson          had been smeared
some generations   ago   she wiped
her tampons                      welling
with sediment    a raven   coursed past
gestured   to a heap     of abortions
putrid and nursling on garlic    stars
this marsh of bones    the raven spat   was
once the place you sought   now         ash
now    swampland   now go         before I
shit your flesh and slop your pus-clot globs
with your matted  eye socket   strings

IMPERIAL EAGLE
PHALACROCORAX
ARISTOTELIS
EUROPEAN SHAG
CREX CREX
CORNCRAKE
CALONECTRIS a
plastic bag caught
in  branches makes
an aeolian lament
percussive  like  losing
BOREALIS CORY'S
SHEARWATERmosq
uito clencher^, sliding
putrescent moon
behind buildings
like shadows
ALSO KNOWN TO
PURSUE AND

almost encircled with woods, among which
partial features of the edifice were seen;——

CATCH AERIAL
PREY SUCH AS

ruffian-like figure / / —all her fortitude was
lost : inexpressible grief and terror ,
emotions of

in mixed light splayed
all   directions
BATS AND MOTHS

☽

greywhite night mist   falling & rising
against   moon among dusk & its phrases
hear blood   rush
bottles smashed how smell
hits   back of the   throat I gave away
my key or did I drop it the event of stairs:
let us rise
& yes I am
falling apart under
towers & yes

I see
moon I see street
lights
moon  lights
light  pink
throwup festoons
sidewalk
& a musical    voice
enters
my ear  break

☽

At about 1630 hours, due
to mysterious explosion
double cabin climbed
over a ruined
part of the adjoining
wall extinct within
about a century
goodbye *the horned*
*moon was set;*
*startled two night*
*birds from the great elm tree*
*between the trees, green pastures and villages ,*
*a glimpse of*
*/ / ran mantling among the broken capitals of*
*columns Presumably, the killed*
*were foreigners*
*watched nightly among*
*the ruins : and to make the story*
*more wonderful, a certain part of the ruin,*
*from whence no person / / had*
*ever returned*

*/ / great bell ? formerly served to announce*
*the arrival of strangers / / long since*
*fallen from its station*

. *22 PERSONS*
*DIED. WAIT*
computer monitor
toppled *ANOTHER*
*VIEW OF THE*
*MOON* corner   under
a tree
whose bark      to your
thoughts
*WANDERING*
*AMONG CLOUDS,*
long
distance  splits
*ABOVE THE*
*JAGGED RIDGES*
dry cleaners sign
blinking but am I
emptier *OF THE*
*STEEPS: THENCE*
than I have ever been/
our lives *YLKN*

*SHRWTR MTCLL*
*FLVYLLWWGTL*
*PYRRHCRX GRCLS*

☽

sate in the park till the    patterns of  spit
moonlight \\tis perceived    on sidewalk  glistening
profusion of game : gazed mildly :    icily *confusion and*
They were strangers to man!    *tumult , a scene of:*

☽

imperfectly the gloomy abyss beyond;——saw : her    *NOW HGHTND BY*
aunt, the corpse of    *SHTTRD*

*full moon* goodbye    *BATTLEMENTS*

☽

*I went up with them as far as the*    DEMOLISHED
*blacksmith's, a fine lovely moonlight*    WALLS  O
*nightUSDRONE*    branches in

☽

It nests in holes in trees or buildings, in a cliff,
quarry, rock outcrops

*THE HUGE MASSES*
*OF RUIN // NOW*

*a little winding way cut in the rock among*
*thickets of dwarf wood*

*SILENT AND*
*GRASS GROWN* a

*Other prey taken according to availability and*
*includes birds to the size of ptarmigans, ducks*
*and medium-sized geese, occasionally fish,*
*amphibians, crustaceans and beetles*
[][][][][]rot rot rot rot rot*The nest consists of*
*a scrape sometimes lined with grass or leaves*
*and is found under the shelter of bushes or*
*overhanging grasses missile attack*
*mainly rocky country with cliffs and ravines,*
*caves, patches of woodland, scattere*USDRONE*d*
*trees or groves*
QUERQUEDULA GARGANEY
GALLINAGO MEDIA GREAT SNIPE
RMPSLTR MNGLCS MNGLN FNCH
PHYLLSCPS SNDNS

sagging boy with mind
in ferment sat
corroding the night
he trapped a bird in a
silver wire basket asked
her how do you fly
above the leaves
above the bounds of
night teach me so that I
may reach the
moon that beckoning
tumor she squeaked her
beak would not speak
so he ripped off her
wings left her sickening

MNTN CHFFCHFF

in the slop

SYLVIA SARDA MARMORA'S WARBLER
PARUS PALUSTRIS MARSH
TIT
SYLV MLNCPHL SRDNN WRBLR
LCSTLL LSCNDS SV'S WRBLR

of her veins he found a
leech gatherer hands
hideous
with worms he met her
slavering on the sands

MRGLLS LBLLS SMW PLCTRPHNX
NVLS SNW BNTNG

he wreaked a
pandemonium

☽

*At about 2045 hours, US*   on her draining dugs
*Drone targeted a tube well*   next he breathed a

*At about*   night mist slinking low
*1255 hours, US drone struck two cars*   along the shore he

☽

*nest is a shallow scrape on ground, usually in*   coughed and gagged tell me
*slightly elevated site providing a good view*   he said how to

*PASSED UNDER WOODS, SHADE OF*
*THE , TO THE EDIFICE WE HAD THE*
*CRESCENT MOON WITH THE AULD*
*MOON IN HER ARMS COME*
*BACK OIL POLLUTION (OIL SPILLS)*
*IN MOULTING AND PRE-*
*MIGRATIONAL STAGING AREAS,*
*COLLISIONS WITH POWERLINES and*
*wind turbines, lead poisoning as a result of lead shot*
*and fishing weight ingestion during migration and*
*on wintering grounds*
*gigantic remains of an NEST / / flourished*
*and decayed with the building / / remaining*
*branches, leafless and moss-grown*
*frequent almost as the leaves*


*One missile was fired*
beyond, lemon and orange

float ethereal
up to the moon his
gore swelled him the
night mist made moss
of his mass an
ugly corpse all pocked
and speckled with
craters almost they said
like the face of the
turgid moon whose
light   embrace do you
gleam     such silver
& so
otherworldly  car jumps
the curb  store signs

flow freely
phantasmic  spirit

☾

T BT 2050 HRS, S DRN CRRD T. MSSL *sun sink below those*
STRK 'T *hills," said she, "or*

WHCH SH CLD NT GZ PNWTH *illumine this take-out*
NDFFRNC *scene! // sunk*

'TTCK NVLLG CVLN *perhaps, in misery!"*

☽

wait the drive-thru *moon retired again,*  grocery bags laden
*appeared and disappeared several times*  & empty & *abandonment*
*before I reached home*  *of traditional agro-pastoral*

*beyond, lemon and orange , groves of / /*  *activities, reduced*
*fruit glowing*  *connectivity between*

*nests in holes in trees, cliffs, buildings*  tattered
*and steep river banks.*  at a traffic light

☽

drone *a flightless bird that lived in shrublands and*
*open\*\*( fieldsextinction was likely caused by*
*introduced rats and cats*

*bt, s clmbd th mss, th mn cm t frm bhnd mntn*
*mss f blck clds wt*
*the [femm]male performs an undulating courtship*
*flight; a series of flaps followed by glide with wings*
*held in dihedral.*

*shriek swoop // open valley // tall groves of*
*cypress pine & poplar // ruined villa*
*sometimes // broken columns between the*
*branches of a pine //* a creature a woman
do you fear her bodysmell the weeping of
her sores she is wringing
hands turning one over the other as though
to make a frothing sign her hair
her eyes
she sees inward at the edge of the woods
twilight falls the swarms of egg laying
creatures begins to nestle
she shrieks a hex you ruin she you shriek
shrieks never sleep again moonpale impaled
on treebranches clust'ring sharp
moonflesh knotted shine

you text, hunched
*metapopulations, disturbance,*
*poaching,*

over the screen yellow
square flat
glowing empty
*unsustainable hunting,*
*extreme climatic events,*

empty lot    cigarette
stubs lodged in
streetcar *hybridisation*
*with released captive-bred*
*Chukar and Red-legged*
*Partridge,* tracks look
back  look back lights
dim *and the transfer of*
*pathogens and parasites* &
yellowed through
tinted glass shadows
*from these species*
HUNTED FOR
THEIR FEATHERS
moving & recombining
someone runs stops

fang vision spell
*on the carcass stem*

some came up/down to the street to put
ears hands noses to the stone made : flesh to sense
in their ways what way was made what way what*

fang vision spell
cluck chirrup corpse


: flesh said PDEEER #(*ditus* / "indu / its per) said
"everyw" said (mutati / take th / main to / ncreases)

what shudder took I/them how we/you received


lighted caves : (*sen* / ng a *sen*) what dancing spoke :
howl & eeew cack-cack-cackle grackle dances blue black

sheen of feather yo whoo shriek is what the shadows do

fang vision spell
chirrup cluck corpse flower chew

(percep / se in / on, it / ) when what unmade was (veryth / )
boom-clang bark, coo you cooling breath
break you couthed call (I) think (we) see dncng particles gone : SOUND

man broke off his finger (hcild) fell silent wheeeoo
dog ate her (taiel) you left your golden string then
on the street wrenched it from your scalp exuding pus chew-rit

bridge

horses' hooves

turned gravel

nest, so many

in a leaning

light

remember

gravel path

under leaning

nests, so many

trees, many


crooked wooden

remember

path

sticks

tree, many

low

the horses' hooves

heavy and huge

sticks turned thin

slats the sound

light


slats the sound

the road turned thin

heavy and huge

low

life

slats the sound

turned sound

bridge

remember

crooked wooden

turned gravel

☽

*At about 0525 hours, US Drone carried*   AND
*out missile strike*   SLAUGHTERED AS

YTHY FLGL TFTD DCK   running headlights
STRX RLNSS RL WL   on a parked car

LYRRS MLKSWCZ CCSN GRS TTRGLLS   PESTS, THE LAST
CCSCS CCSN SNWCCK   REPORTED

*sun set : it set with uncommon splendour*   all the front wheels
*/ / threw a fiery gleam athwart /— woods*   have been stolen
*ruins , some scattered fragments of the*   sidewalk SIGHTING

☽

*picturesque ruin part of seen partially ?*　　sidewalk　speckled &
*among foliage*　　pocked　by

*Drone attacked a House in 09 05 09 The dead*　　**sadness** *these courts, silence*
*persons includedabout 2010 hours*　　*and gloom of [*

*grey stone, in the heavy Saxon-gothic style*　　*occupied as it was .*

☽

*ncrsd mchnztn f frms hs mnt th lss f mprtnt frgng*
*sts, sch s stckyrds nd stbls, nd th lss f bndnd frm*
*bldngs stbl fr nst-sts. rgnchlrn pstcds n 1950s nd*
*1960s nd rdntcds n 1970s nd 1980s hd dsstrs ffcts n*
*mny wl ppltns n rp, prtclrly nrth-wst rp IN THE*
*EVENING, UNCONFIRMED*
*REPORTS INDICATE THAT US*
*DRONE CARRIED OUT MISSILE*
*STRIKE IN VILLAGE NO DETAILS*
*ARE AVAILABLE.*

*The species mostly migratory and nomadic*

its pores steam
out    dreams *with*
*more mournful ideas*
*/ / ; she scarcely heard*
of cold    sleep
a conflicting   wind
*goodbye the moon*
*appearing, now half*
*veiled,*   buffets me
pulls   wrong times out

of an    unremembering

70

☽

*the moon travelled through the clouds, tinging them*
*yellow as she passed along, with two stars near her,*
*one larger than the other* come back
*obscurity of the greater part of the pile*
*heightened its sublimity, and led fancy on*
*to scenes of horror*

chime moon & I
and now retired behind
heavy clouds,
start   spooked by
what  looming
future the stars still

☽

diffused a romantic gloom around
GELOCHELIDON NILOTICA
COMMON GULL-BILLED TERN
UPUPA EPOPS COMMON HOOPOE
WD NTHTCH TRNG GLRL WD
SNDPPR PHYLLSCPS SBLTRX
hpauemaost ostrlgeusa asuirean
tsrtyeoachcer inalus torubeixc
great grey ekirsh
HYDROBATES CASTRO BAND-
RUMPED STORM-PETREL
ALECTORIS BARBARA
BARBARY PARTRIDGE
REGULUS MADEIRENSIS MADEIRA
KINGLET COLUMBA TROCAZ
MADEIRA LAUREL-PIGEON
CPRMLGS RFCLLS RD-NCKD
NGHTJR PHLRPS LBTS
RD-NCKD PHLRP
ANAS PLATYRHYNCHOS MALLARD
PUFFINUS PUFFINUS MANX
SHEARWATER
HIERAAETUS PENNATUS BOOTED
EAGLE HIPPOLAIS CALIGATA
BOOTED WARBLER

t bt 1000 hrs, tw pckps wr ttckd wth tw
rckts frm nknwn dstntn (Drn ttck) 15 11 15

"THISTLE SHOOK ;
MOSS ;WIND" pain
gaping  bearing
down I am falling  A
GOTHIC GATE,
RICHLY  apart on a
street corner I   said
ORNAMENTED W
FRET-WORK
WAIT I  wrote
you an email  THESE
SOON CLOSED IN,
reflection of one tower
in the glass
of another tower:
CONTRACTING
THE DIMENSIONS
decomposes I look
back at her looking
back & forever
OF THE MOON
WITHOUT
we've lost each
other spirits
CONCEALING HER

pour down the sides
of the towers & WAIT

☽

"the lord was angry with me    our lives patterns
because of you" while the    of  spit  on
*moon just setting*    sidewalk  glistening
*as we reached home* goodbye    icily  O branches


*a fine moonlight night* goodbye


*Nine dead were local targeted*
*American Drone. Further*
*details are awaited.*


☽

NTHS TRVLS TR PPT BCNTS GTHGNS
TRMPTR FNCH
LARUS CACHINNANS CASPIAN GULL
BUBULCUS IBIS CATTLE EGRET
CEPPHUS GRYLLE BLACK GUILLEMOT
FRINGILLA MONTIFRINGILLA
BRAMBLING

CLDRS LB SNDRLNG THLSSS
SNDVCNSS SNDWCH TRN

*had been suffered, ancient as it was, to sink into ruins .*

⟩

// lonely and deserted air //
melancholy awe, emotions of
also threatened by oil and gas exploration
an acid claps
two carcasses together their clay
swacks
sticks & flaps
as it smacks look
who rends
a wall a flaccid heart
flays a newt when the ghost
enters
the
room
cold
claps down
dead hands
the cat
goes bolting away

IT WAS A
MOONLIGHT
NIGHT you walk past
but just in a memory
MOON ROSE at the
corner everyone
LARGE AND DULL,
LIKE AN ILL-
CLEANED BRASS
PLATE, bends into
lighted screens scapes
swept  hot
air SLOWLY
—SURMOUNTS THE
HAZE, bellows
clacking resounding
underground
we all   rush into
FAINT BRIGHT

☽

*window opened upon a romantic glade* / /    changing intersection
*roved among woody recesses* / / *groves ,*    we all rush into
*lengthened pomp of*    changing    wind picks


*on grey walls, moss* / / *pointed windows of*    me up sets
*the chapel : ivy and briony hung : a fantastic*    *T BT 1745 HRS, TW*
*wreath* : a bog : of blood    *DRN TTCKS WR*

*passed on to the court of entrance, but*    *CRRD T N VLLG*
*paused again* / / *branching from it, ran*    *MNDWM ND NSHP*
*along the brow of a precipice*    me down/ on the
*ftn lngrd bhnd th prty* / / *dstnt lndscp* / /    other side    moon
/ / *drk flg f frgrnd*    takes a turn writing

75

*stumbled over : broken pavement & her*    some words they
*voice returned [was] in hollow echoes :*    garble time
                     *more terrific*    *SHKT R F THSL*

☽

*Venus almost like another moon* goodbye    gesture ill

*their brightness seemed concentrated, (half-*    illumination   a spark
*moon)*    floats down *AT*
*are awaited.*    *ABOUT 2050 HOURS*

☽

RUINS OF A FABRIC WHICH HAD
ONCE BEEN A CASTLE // POINT OF
ROCK THAT OVERHUNG ?A DEEP
VALLEY; // BROKEN TURRETS
RISING *WOODS THAT EMBOSOMED
IT, HEIGHTENED THE
OBJECT, PICTURESQUE BEAUTY OF

US DRONE
CARRIED OUT from
a decomposing
cigarette & this burn
flaking MISSILE
STRIKES AT TWO
DIFFERENT THE

ONLY ONCE WHILE WE WERE IN
THE WOOD, THE MOON BURST
THROUGH THE INVISIBLE VEIL
WHICH ENVELOPED HER, THE
SHADOWS OF THE OAKS
BLACKENED, AND THEIR LINES
BECAME MORE STRONGLY
MARKED COME BACK

MOON HAD THE
OLD MOON IN HER
ARMS, soft un
illuminating light the
sign BUT NOT SO
PLAIN TO BE SEEN
AS THE NIGHT of its
unmaking enters

☽

meet us in the heinous     me my blood
hollow ]]where remains chafe     *moving, the roads very*

*the eastern tower, , huge fragments*     *dirty* yearning & falling
*of / / almost demolished : scattered*     & the towers press &
*amid high grass*     reach  into night's

☽

*loose stone tott'ring o'er*  illumination ill
*trembling shade."*  NIGHTJAR

*a huge wingless, carnivorous diving bird with teeth*  FICEDULA qaailu

Petals stuck struck & splayed on murky glass: sun a dust in the lungs.
Where spell shudders your fingers. Here it goes watch closely: irregular
turn. Path of wood rings ring worms ringing steel bells.

"Officer-involved shooting" means mouths were unhinged hinges creaking
at night.

Here it goes watch closely: take down the town take the looping wires
down take the rooftops and their shining shingles take the windows
windows shining in the town take the posters the banana stands the china
cups chipped computer chips take them computers with them take them
down to the ground.

Blare snare.

Chairs suddenly fall over all the chairs there were falling fell.

Three women hunched close, gesticulating. A nodding branch knows. What
thought: the crow.

Time is what life leaks, leaves behind.

Pipes and vents maze the walls: follow them.

A rooted gate goes flying, smacks a lamppost which also flies, both go
lurching out of sight, down on the night the lurching lamppost casts a
careening sheen.

A dizzy sheen frazzles and flummoxes ones who walk below their
merriment: does it falter.

"Shots were fired."

"Officer-involved shooting" means juniper berries out of my chewed
mouth.

What is the ground but what the ground fells ground falls ground down groaning.

What was the ground but what I threw down: gently swaying light fixtures, plastic geraniums, accordion keys, Punch's glass eye, the beat (beat beat).

What was ground down took the ground up streaming, screaming dirt from pockets and pores whose blood was window bright.

And ground what was. What was. What bore down, what bears. Bear the ground now, how ground.

Windows bright whose shards shone: new light light without sense sense blaring sense blooming: riot.

The moon is a yellowing bruise but "Officer-involved shooting" enchanted the bystanders. Windows whose berries brightened the day, berries whose blush brightened up the penises. Who are you wearing, no really.

Paint falls off in flakes, circular scuffs on the ground, tire streaks, whose cheeks peeked.

"Officer-involved shooting" but all they want is to die, have died, are dying.

Three umbrellas: two open.

Shut the fuck up.

Rain in the puddles and puddles in the mouths.

More people are alive now than have ever died. Or: more rats were born today than bats died yesterday.

The dead speak by rubbing their noses against glass leaving grease on the pane slamming doors fussing with their ribbons their trappings shadows fidgeting generally the dead speak by signs and they go like this watch closely: a creak a beak sometimes in the mirror a thing will move, sinister. Room of tables at crooked angles. All fall down.

You will never really know what it feels like but when the inanimate call: chorus of dust. I mean the dust in your nose is a song bless you. "Officer-involved shooting" means the mouth is speaking for itself clattering against my wooden teeth. "Officer-involved shooting" means I want to hear you say it, go ahead.

Rock: throw it. Window: already smashed. When the rock face runs live with avalanching dirt rootless, the sound is applause, dry grasp of the damned. Dust.

Dust in the lungs: are the petals slipping. Are they rotting, stinking in the moist fumes of morning sun.

A hungry person holds a bun wrapped in plastic the plastic gleams gives off an itching sticky and pulling stink a hungry dog sits down. The sign for spell arrives at your doorstep, the stamp a hand in a jug of blood.

Would you take a picture of us standing under this shadow.

Would you hold this while I take a shit.

I was doing fine until I remembered about the stampede. Up came the rosebeds up bled the crows heads you were known to talk in your sleep but in death you just stared. Sometimes in the mirror: sinister.

Rune was ruin in the avalanche sun.

It doesn't really happen any other time. Just a minute.

(Shake down the wall.) In rubble under rubble you will find a bird a poster
a banana stand china cups chipped. (Bat the bird away.) Egg in rubble.
(Leave the egg.) Beside the egg look closely catch the glimmer of a key.
(Wedge the key into your fist.) Open hole. (Open ground.) Open hole in
the ground. (Fall into the hole.) In the hole you will feel cold. (Seize the
cold.) Take in the cold.

(In the cold find dark.) In dark the wall. (Rip up the wall rip it by the roots
with your teeth roots of your teeth rip it.) Your teeth will wrench out torn.
(Flick them bleeding marbles at the wall.) Then the wall will fall in rubble
under rubble will open a flight of stairs. (Descend them.)

Under the stairs the bird waits beaked. (Fend it off with the cold coiled
under your tongue.) Rubble sprouts by night. (Down rubble roots go
shooting.) Avoid the shoots for they will branch and dance you. (Vein
you new pin and pain you slew through.) Trash burns. (Smell it.) Egg has
hatched. (Hatched a computer.) Hatched another key. (Hatched a tooth
clawing.)

petals in what teeth


glass Blare: this falling stared. also
ground runs over wooden falls itching

                    but dust have your shining maze a morning
                    hold move, ribbons known bore two struck

    now chipped bright. And the fuck stinking
    gleams of gesticulating. holding up

behind. Pipes until you. Dust
smacks already goes up. in their watch the

                    fells knows. fussing below bless there the
                    the means the the geraniums, the day,

                    splayed Whose bruise than worms plastic
                    pockets the fidgeting the doing you. means

              bats peeked. "Officer-involved off minute.
              cheeks were talk leaks, casts hungry

lamppost shadow. are and means mirror:
whose me is dust. inanimate sense it

fixtures, Shut with bystanders. Windows
really picture chips died. person down &

              crow. Time in lives are Path Chairs lurching
              was a sense the light crows eye, an it

petals in what teeth. ringing from any and
what posters stink avalanche in you

              us go night while face The bun
              yellowing beat) (beat. What to umbrellas: stamp

the sometimes close, Bear clattering
just china they down does up sun.

sense the nodding computer shingles was
down he ground town back a down of light

the arrives speak leaves a shooting"
really leaves the stained but happen the born

feels damned. dog wooden of Who down on
pores never I the die, means

moist stampede. in wrapped bells. and light
watch mean in slipping. shit. The the grasp

brightened take dry of but like shoot
doorstep, both on a a ruin streaming, down,

dust but the clicks falls Just out murky
plastic snare smashed. ground them more

irregular gate angles. stolen sound song
whose what leaving grease ground of me

I in take shooting" down: at down blood.
Would sticky enchanted hear in blood. is

women down. You other out in All all fine
they are careening goes glass to now, I

was goes ring were red. Rain people which
wood by a closely: white no in take A shoot

itself spell moon beat, fall in in rock spell
life slamming rotting, sight, chorus crooked

I merriment: "Officer-involved mouth the
I is take computers what rosebeds

want time. Window: juniper dead shone:
Paint will you of berries take it. A Or: Up

What Would berries will pane chairs died,
flummoxes shortcut creak whose your

night. Here Here What Petals ground
suddenly Sometimes the Room flies,

hunched are this me. the groaning. What
banana by whose walls: a tables it stands

keys, your like want to drain take the the
mouth. What the blush of bowl he sits

vents was. yesterday. a down against
shooting" glass bright throw thought:

fumes like closely: the the "Officer-involved
lamppost is is the my call: applause, of dirt

and he who walk sheen ground, branch I
Punch's and take were sound but nose

blaring falter. "Shots is speaking take ahead.
Rock: hungry penises. takes town unhinged,

rings hinges circular dead new closely: took
when the the all "Officer-involved the

follow fell. Three a watch tire for
today in cups beautiful heads it, signs fell

noses death windows puddles know like creaking
was. swaying shadows died thing in

avalanching steel wearing, what shudders
them. A gives it, ever riot. The

you and off flying sun the the what gum
fingers. are Beaks stolen generally doors rats

the man berries you bled window lurching but
lungs. sheen. A really. have with sign is

sleep is ground the stuck is go with ground
lungs: a goes flakes, this at shining bright

streaks, take in ground turn. a plastic blood
the ducks and brightened up jug them

sinister. Rune The mouths. More puddles
down. sun. remembered whose against

fired." "Officer-involved in down aisle
under chewed dying. Three windows it of a

, hand dirt on them in my beak
doesn't alive screaming were bobbing came

they live looping mirror What out dizzy
blooming: trappings accordion without for

shooting" you scuffs rooftops ground.
Windows wind go of speak ones

frazzles rootless, say holds threw shooting"
your pulling chewing gently standing

rooted shooting" shards rubbing "Officer-
involved Are mouths how about ground

sinister. When ground. bears. was the has
open. was Dust. A

wires wall.) in open your chipped. cold. (In
(Hatched rubble slew Your with shooting.)

closely (Vein shoots your hatched. (Hatched
rubble in In hole.) the teeth has bleeding

stand (Shake by (Smell the Will will of pin
they roots it Egg marbles wrench wall

into poster (Down hole. (Flick stairs the rip
it.) rubble rip wall. flight for the open key.

will wall.) rubble teeth (Leave branch
hole cold. another Take Will the them

computer.) cold under.) feel key cold. by roots find bird
Then the them.) Under in key.) wall dark

Egg ground.) egg and dark your coiled.) at the fall
beaked. china in it.) will you. rubble. (Will a

night. key your cold (Rip a Hatched you
the banana open fist.) burns. Trash tooth

you under it with down cups (Take the
stairs. egg.) the the off will ground. the

new of dance the the rubble Rubble teeth In
and you (Fall (Descend glimmer Beside

Avoid (Wedge away.) (Bat you up bird
pain your hole waits torn. under on go

out find a through.) (Fend catch In
bird roots look sprouts clawing.) of open

fang vision spell
chew noise chirrup cluck

they / we took the message with deva (take / th)-station knewwe didn't (be
/ its) have enough silk splels to give flesh sound became CHEW
BARK nbeara) sound became blood on the street

blood was (e / alterat / shes co / are sent / of death) PDEEER
branch torn want (wane) branching (sleeping) some
said blood too (can / and "se / cease t / Can) can speak

fang vision spell
corpse flower bland
wreathe rotten tendrilss

said TRILL , BREER , hiss yap-yip yap  will-will said
hiss his said this said conscious said (un) (sun) (sung) skin close
d then b e c a ( m e ) s t ( o n ( e a g ) a ) i n ( b u ( t

HOOT SING NOTE CRY WHIT CHIRRUP
( c r ( a c k ) e d n o ) w ( & l e a ) k i n g
CHEER-UP , l e a c ( h i n g & WHIT HOO GRIG-GRIG

fang vision spell
corpse chirrup

(xtrem / acqui / utatio / clear / mute t
be / cle) ROAR YO { wreng*hched wher ther feat
hers ther re(ad red read –kewp felt (w/here)

NOTE

In the poems marked ☽, all italicized language is quoted, rewritten, condensed, and scrambled from the following four sources:

Ann Radcliffe, *The Mysteries of Udolpho*

Dorothy Wordsworth, *Grasmere Journals*

the IUCN Red List of Threatened Species: http://www.iucnredlist.org

a leaked document from the Pakistani government, reporting CIA drone strikes dating from 2006 to the present, and available through the Bureau of Investigative Journalism: https://www.thebureauinvestigates.com/stories/2014-01-29/get-the-data-pakistani-governments-secret-report-on-drone-strikes

Quotations from Radcliffe tend to cluster around the word "ruin," from Wordsworth around the word "moon," from the IUCN Red list around the word "nest," and from the Pakistani government report around the word "drone."

The quotation on page 29, "hearts burning," is from Luke 24:32.

The quotation on page 73, "the lord was angry with me because of you," is from Deuteronomy 4:21.

Acknowledgments

I am deeply grateful to everyone at Omnidawn for bringing this book
into the world: to Gillian Hamel and Ken Keegan; to Cassandra Smith
for her vision; and to Rusty Morrison for editing these pages with
insight, compassion, and questioning so intuitive that revision felt like
collaboration. Thanks to Steve Halle for helping with the design.

Thank you to the editors & readers of the journals where versions of these
poems first appeared: Muriel Leung and Joey De Jesus (*Apogee*, and online
in *Perigree*); 최 Lindsay, Segen Gebrehiwet, and Kelsey Liu (*Berkeley Poetry
Review*, and the chapbook-style anthology *MIDTERM*); Zachary Evans
(*Calamity*); Bükem Reitmayer, Aba Micah Collins-Sibley, and Ann Ward
(*Cosmonauts Avenue*); Carolina Ebeid and Bin Ramke (*Denver Quarterly*); Lily
Duffy and Rachel Levy (*DREGINALD*); Christopher Patrick Miller and Lyn
Hejinian (*FLOOR*); Brenda Mann Hammack (*Glint*); Nate Wilkerson, Emily
Alex, and Evan Lavender-Smith (*Puerto del Sol*); Alexandra Kamerling (*The
Rational*); Steve Halle (*Spoon River Poetry Review*).

Thanks to David Wilson, Larry Rinder and Kathy Geritz for featuring a
part of this book in their Way Bay exhibition at the Berkeley Art Museum
and Pacific Film Archive.

Many thanks to Lyn Hejinian for believing in this book from the beginning.
Thanks also to all of the friends, teachers and mentors who read the
manuscript while it was in progress, and who gave support, advice,
conversation, and insight, especially CA Conrad, Brandon Brown, Cecil
Giscombe, Jane Gregory, Hoa Nguyen, Alice Notley, Geoffrey G. O'Brien,
Emily Wolahan.

Thank you to the beloved ones whose presence sustained & inspired me
during writing of this book, and most of all to Adam & Jeanne Ahmed,
Daniel Benjamin, Seulghee Lee, Ismail Muhammad, Anne & Andrew &
Matthew Stancek, Rasheed Tazudeen.

Claire Marie Stancek is also the author of *MOUTHS* (Noemi, 2017). She edits Nion Editions, a chapbook press. Originally from outside Toronto, Ontario, she now lives in Berkeley, California.

Oil Spell
by Claire Marie Stancek

Cover art: Original artwork by Ruben Briseno Reveles
www.rubenreveles.com

Cover typeface: Kabel LT Std & Perpetua Std
Interior typefaces: Perpetua Std

Cover & interior design by Cassandra Smith

Offset printed in the United States
by Edwards Brothers Malloy, Ann Arbor, Michigan
On 55# Glatfelter B18 Antique
Acid Free Archival Quality Recycled Paper

Publication of this book was made possible in part by gifts from:
The New Place Fund
The Clorox Company Foundation

Omnidawn Publishing
Oakland, California
2018
Rusty Morrison & Ken Keegan, senior editors & co-publishers
Trisha Peck, managing editor & program director
Gillian Olivia Blythe Hamel, senior poetry editor
Cassandra Smith, poetry editor & book designer
Sharon Zetter, poetry editor, book designer & development officer
Liza Flum, poetry editor
Avren Keating, poetry editor & fiction editor
Juliana Paslay, fiction editor
Gail Aronson, fiction editor
Tinia Montford, marketing assistant
Emily Alexander, marketing assistant
Terry A. Taplin, marketing assistant
Matthew Bowie, marketing assistant
SD Sumner, copyeditor